Catch Wrestling

Stepping into

The Snake Pit

By

Daniel DiMarzio

Catch Wrestling, Stepping into the Snake Pit
By Daniel DiMarzio

Published by the *Winds of Japan Shop*

ISBN 9798703390528

Author: Daniel DiMarzio

A special thank you to Snake Pit USA Head Coach Joel Bane and his understudy, Brandon Browne, Head Coach of Modern Martial Arts.

Dedicated to Maya and Marco.

Coach Bane (standing) and Coach Browne (ground)

Warning:

This book is for informational purposes only. None of the information and/or techniques in this book should be practiced or attempted by any person. The information and/or training techniques in this book can cause serious bodily injury or death. The author and publisher assume no responsibility for the use of anything contained in this book.

Contents

Introduction

Martial Arts and the Exotic

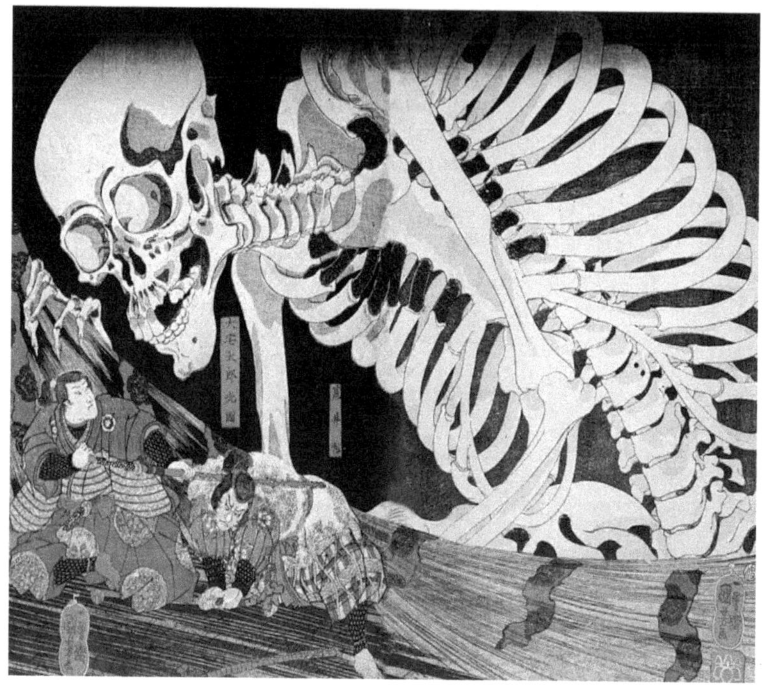

Japanese Painting by Utagawa Kuniyoshi, circa 1800s

As the old saying goes, *"The grass is always greener on the other side."* This is especially true when you add an exotic element into the mix. Historically, when it comes to the *martial arts,* that exotic element has been its link to Asia.

In the West, when many people think of the martial arts their minds immediately wander to China, Japan and Korea. The image of an Asian martial arts master in strange clothing who can move faster than lightning pops into their heads. It is something that has been ingrained in us from a young age through books, movies and games.

Even with the emergence of Mixed Martial Arts (MMA), the image of the Asian martial arts master still exists largely in the public eye. While MMA draws huge crowds of spectators, many of these people are simply fans watching a sporting event.

As an example, I once attended a birthday party. I sat next to a friend I had not seen in a very long time. We began to catch up and the conversation steered toward the martial arts. I was studying Brazilian Jiu-jitsu at the time

(BJJ). He had no idea what that was, so I explained to him that it had to do with the ground fighting you often see in MMA fights.

He chuckled and said he liked to watch cage fights on TV sometimes. Then his ears perked up and he said, "I just saw a movie about Bruce Lee's teacher. Have you seen it?" I said, "No, I'm sorry I didn't catch that one yet." His reply was, "Man, that guy was amazing. If you put him in a cage with ten MMA fighters, he would beat the hell out of all of them."

I sat back in my chair staring at him, waiting for the punch line. It never came. He was a nice enough guy, in his early thirties. He kept on talking about how the old martial arts masters could defeat large groups of men, armed with swords, with their bare hands. If they could do that, surely they could wipe the floor with any martial artist walking around today.

He was so absorbed in telling these stories that I didn't have the heart to argue with him. I also didn't want to cause a scene at the party. I smiled and nodded, noting how amazing the movie must have been. Thus is the power of the media. What many people watch on TV and see in the movies gets turned into reality in their minds.

This is not to say that the Asian influence on the martial arts is not warranted. It most certainly is. There are many amazing martial arts, and martial arts masters, who have come from China, Japan, Korea and so forth. They have influenced modern MMA in a huge way as well. Brazilian Jiu-jitsu, one of the most effective fighting styles out there, has its roots in Japanese Jujutsu and Judo. Muay Thai from Thailand has greatly influenced the standup and clinch game in MMA. There are many other examples as well…but what is often overlooked is the contribution of Western martial arts to fighting.

Take boxing, for example. There are millions of boxing fans out there and boxing is used to train MMA fighters as well. Most people think of it only as a sport, when in fact it is a legitimate martial art that can be used to defend your life.

Wrestling is another example. Many people see it only as a sport and do not think of it as a martial art. However, it has become a cornerstone of MMA. If you are not familiar with takedowns in a fight you are sorely unprepared.

So, why aren't boxing and wrestling considered martial arts by the masses? Sure, they are sports. No one is arguing that, but they can easily be used to defend oneself in a life or death situation. However, to many people in the West, they are missing that "exotic" appeal.

There are no *mysterious rituals* that often accompany martial arts from the East. For the most part, there aren't many *flashy* moves. The training attire is usually plain and straightforward.

However, boxing and wrestling tend to focus specifically on set ways of fighting. With boxing you are using your fists, with wrestling you are taking someone down or preventing yourself from being taken down. Many martial arts from Asia include punching, kicking and joint locks. They have a seemingly endless number of techniques for all types of situations. The techniques can be complicated and look spectacular, especially to the untrained eye.

Even Brazilian Jiu-jitsu (BJJ) has that exotic appeal to it. It's a "Brazilian" martial art with a "Japanese" name (Jiu-jitsu). That alone makes it interesting. Not to mention, it has proven itself to be an extremely effective martial art both in sport and actual combat. Many people flock to train in it.

But what if I told you there was a Western martial art out there few have ever trained in? One that uses many of the same *exotic* Eastern martial arts techniques and couples it with the best techniques from Western combat sports. It's a martial art that was used in MMA matches before anyone even knew what an MMA match was.

This Western martial art, honed and crafted in England starting in the 1490s, developed its own vicious style of fighting. Influenced from fighting techniques picked up worldwide by the British Navy, the art was perfected by fighters in England. It was brutal. It was savage. It was violent.

This style came to be known as "Catch-as-Catch-Can." They didn't use fancy names for their techniques or have bizarre spiritual rituals steeped in tradition. They trained to fight…and they chose to fight in an especially aggressive and brutal fashion meant to cause pain and misery to their adversaries.

Chapter 1

Getting Back to My Roots

For the better part of my life, I have been interested in studying cultures from all around the world. Along with these studies, I have taken an interest in the martial arts and fighting practices produced by these cultures. It is something that has fascinated me and taken me to various places around the world.

It brought me to the other side of the planet, living and working in Japan for approximately two years. While there, I studied Bujutsu with a Japanese master. It has taken me to Latin America, where I spent time in the Dominican Republic. There I did research for a book I wrote about modern day sword duels. Few people realize it, but in the Dominican Republic people still fight with swords (machetes) on a regular basis. These barbaric fights happen often there, sometimes ending with people being maimed or killed.

After returning to America (from Japan), I picked up Brazilian Jiu-jitsu for a period of time. I found an amazing school with an incredible teacher near my home. I believe Brazilian Jiu-jitsu is one of the best martial arts in the world for fighting and I enjoyed the classes very much.

The realities of life set in however, and I found myself struggling to make it to the classes. I became so busy with work, school and starting a family that I wasn't able to make it to the gym as much as I would have liked. I decided not to sign up for another contract at the school. I told myself once my situation calmed down I would return.

In the meantime, I trained whenever I could with friends or family. I worked out alone quite a bit. I also began training my young daughter by incorporating moves while we played. It was a game to her and she loved it. I took what I liked and found useful from the various martial arts I had studied and focused on that. Before I knew it, my wife was pregnant again and my family was continuing to grow.

During my hectic schedule my mind never drifted far from the martial arts. Up until this point, my interest had mainly been in Japanese martial arts. I had studied Japanese Jujutsu before moving to Japan. I had spent time in Japan learning Bujutsu and had come home and trained in Brazilian Jiu-jitsu. But all of these martial arts really didn't pertain to my own personal background or heritage.

I am an American of European descent. Most of my bloodline comes from Italy and Ireland. I don't know if having children brought it on me, but I suddenly became very interested in my background. I spent a lot of time in Asia during my life…and was obsessed with Japan for quite a while. Now, I wanted to learn more about Europe and, following my pattern in the past, more about the martial arts from there.

One day, I came across a story online. An MMA fighter named Josh Barnett had competed in a grappling match against Dean Lister. Dean Lister was a BJJ expert, considered one of the best grapplers in the world, who had not been submitted in a grappling competition in some sixteen years. Josh Barnett was a Mixed Martial Arts champion.

Now, BJJ is not MMA and vice versa. Just because someone is a world champion in Brazilian Jiu-jitsu does not mean he will be successful in Mixed Martial Arts. The opposite is also true, just because someone is a Mixed Martial Arts champion does not mean he will win a BJJ competition.

So, the match up intrigued me. A world-class BJJ expert versus a world-class MMA fighter…in a pure grappling match. It is safe to say that most people thought that Dean Lister, the expert in Brazilian Jiu-jitsu, would readily win the match. Why? Brazilian Jiu-jitsu is widely thought of as the best grappling art the planet has ever seen. It has proven itself time and time again in competition and on the street. In a strictly only-grappling match, most would pick BJJ. Not to mention that Dean Lister is a master at it and hadn't been submitted in recent memory.

Josh Barnett, the MMA fighter, obviously knew how to grapple as well. You would have to, if you are a champion MMA fighter. In fact, he had won numerous grappling tournaments. However, he stepped onto the mats representing a little known form of grappling...*Catch Wrestling*. Most people in the grappling world know little if anything about Catch Wrestling. To them, Catch Wrestling would have little chance of defeating the well-established Brazilian Jiu-jitsu art in a situation such as this.

I found the YouTube video of the match and pressed play. Josh Barnett was dressed as a classic wrestler. He had the classic wrestling tights, no shirt, wrestling shoes and socks with Japanese flags on them. His opponent, Dean Lister, had the normal attire for BJJ No-Gi grapplingshorts, rashguard and no shoes.

The match was set to last twenty minutes, with no breaks. For anyone that has ever grappled, that can be an eternity. From the outset of the match, Barnett dominated. He continued to dominate the entire way through the twenty minutes, many times almost landing fight-ending submissions. Lister looked frustrated and extremely uncomfortable.

With only about thirteen seconds left on the clock, Barnett submitted Lister and won the match. The whole match was impressive, but what was even more impressive is *what* he submitted his opponent with. Barnett had side-control and grabbed his opponent in what looked like the classic wrestler's head lock.

This was a move I was repeatedly told *not* to do while I practiced BJJ. I was told it was a bad position, wouldn't work, and it could easily lead to my back being taken. Yet, right before my eyes, I saw one of the best grapplers in the world being submitted by it.

Barnett was in side-control, had grabbed his opponent's head and arm *closest* to him in an s-grip, and sat out cranking the hold. There was no apparent choke set in and people wondered what in the hell he had done to get the submission.

Most people thought it had to be a tap from a neck-crank, and a neck-crank set in deep enough can turn into a choke as well. However, what most people didn't realize was Barnett was putting his opponent into a diaphragm choke. He was crushing his opponent's lungs, literally…while sitting out and putting his entire body weight on him. It is like a python constricting its prey, they breathe out and the hold gets tighter and you cannot take another breath in. Eventually you will suffocate. It doesn't look like the normal choke or strangle (around the neck) however, so people had no idea what he was doing.

After the match, Barnett graciously acknowledged his competitor's skills and then attributed his own success to…*Catch Wrestling.*

That was it. I was hooked and I needed to find out more about this *Catch Wrestling*. About how it came from Europe, specifically England. I had heard whispers about this art before, but never knew what to really make of it.

Chapter 2

The Search

While there are various definitions of what Catch Wrestling actually is, the term basically refers to the practice of catching any hold that you possibly can. According to Snake Pit USA Co-Founder and Head Coach John Potenza, in his article, *The Original No Holds Barred Fighting*, "In old Lancashire England, *catch-as-catch-can* was translated to *catch me if you can*."

Wrestling and fighting techniques from Asia and the Middle East were brought to England by the British Navy. This was mixed with techniques already being practiced in England. These included techniques brought from Ireland and other parts of Europe, and even wrestling moves said to be practiced by the Vikings. The Englishmen of the day took these moves and made them their own. This was Catch-as-Catch-Can Wrestling, or for short, "*Catch*."

Sifting through the enormous amount of information related to Catch Wrestling is not easy. I have been around the martial arts long enough to know you must find a skilled, competent teacher to learn from. A teacher who has a solid, verifiable history and knows *how* to teach.

Many martial arts (the majority) use belts to track an individual's progress. There is usually a way to track down who their teacher was and where they came from. Catch Wrestling does not use a belt system. Its history has become muddled for several reasons. For example, in early matches the Catch Wrestlers were actually fighting each other. There could be numerous different rules to a fight, or absolutely no rules at all. This was all agreed upon beforehand.

These fights could last for an extreme period of time, especially once the fight hit the ground. The grapplers would wrestle to find a submission or an opening, while many of the fans watching would become bored. If both grapplers were extremely skilled, this could seemingly go on forever.

By the time television rolled around, people became wise to what the crowds wanted. The fix was in. Fights became staged events, pleasing the crowds and helping the fighters prolong their careers by avoiding injuries. This gave birth to the modern, staged wrestling seen on television today. Hundreds of years of real fights went out the window and morphed into TV drama.

Ironically, a similar thing happened to grappling when MMA came to America in the 1990s. Fights would end up on the ground, lasting for what seemed like forever, while the fans booed. The promoters quickly made rules to stand the fighters back up to please the crowds.

Now, getting back to searching for a Catch Wrestling school, the task was a difficult one. With Catch Wrestling matches turning into staged events, the real Catch Wrestlers were largely phased out. Their places were taken by the more charismatic entertainers. The public couldn't tell the difference if someone was faking it or really knew how to fight. This literally almost killed Catch Wrestling, making it obsolete. You no longer needed to know how to fight to make money, you just had to be good at pretending how to fight to please the crowds.

So, the Catch Wrestlers dwindled. There was no formalized way to keep track of who trained with whom. Because it was not tied in with religion or mysticism, there was little record kept of it as with other martial arts.

Regardless, I started my search in 2015. Technology is a beautiful thing, but it can also be hard to wade through all the misinformation out there. When it comes to Catch Wrestling, there is plenty of it.

Warnings of charlatans were around every corner. I would find a source or teacher I thought was legitimate, only to find out that they had no credentials whatsoever. As with many of the martial arts, fraudsters were always looking to make a buck off the naïve.

I found some good historical information. It was interesting, but I wanted to find a place to train. I thought the chances were slim to none. At this point, I was really jaded and thought the odds of finding some place near me would be futile.

Then my research went in another direction. I knew of a legendary MMA fighter named Kazushi Sakuraba. He was infamous for defeating many members of the Gracie family, known as some of the best fighters and grapplers on the planet. The Gracies were famous for their Brazilian Jiu-jitsu, which changed the martial arts world. They were fierce fighters who were especially adept at ground fighting.

Sakuraba had managed to defeat several prominent members of the family, many times beating them at their own game on the ground. He did it without using Brazilian Jiu-jitsu. I had heard of him but never knew what he used to help him win his fights.

While doing research, I learned he had actually used *Catch Wrestling*. Well, common-sense kicked in and I figured he had to have learned from a legitimate teacher. Who had taught this man Catch Wrestling?

His name was Billy Robinson and he was a legend in the Catch world. He was an original member of the Snake Pit in England and was considered one of their best practitioners. He had won numerous titles all over the world during his lifetime. He was the real deal. One of the last great Catch Wrestlers of his time.

Learning all this was great, but I still didn't have any way of meeting him. Sadly, I discovered he had passed away in 2014.

I thought to myself, besides Sakuraba, who else did he train? I learned he had contact with Josh Barnett, the MMA fighter and winner of the grappling tournament I had previously researched. I also learned he had trained someone within driving distance of my home.

He lived an hour and a half away, but I was willing to make the trip. I wanted to see if he could show me what real Catch Wrestling looked like. I was skeptical and optimistic at the same time.

His name was Joel Bane. The more I learned about him, the more I felt I had found the right person. He was a Brazilian Jiu-jitsu Black Belt, Catch Wrestler and MMA fighter. He had verifiable ties to Billy Robinson.

I knew I had to meet him. I made contact and an appointment time was set.

Chapter 3

Lessons with a Master

The name of the school was *Modern Martial Arts* in Englishtown, New Jersey. It was the East Coast headquarters of *Snake Pit USA*. I lived in a town just outside of Philadelphia, Pennsylvania, and the drive would take me about an hour and a half.

My work often brought me to New Jersey. I would also go there in the summer with my family, spending days at the beach and fishing. However, the school was located in an area I had never been before. I had passed by the exit that led to the town on the turnpike recently. I was heading to New York City to have lunch with a former student visiting from Japan. That was the closest I had ever come to Englishtown, New Jersey.

Walking into a martial arts gym you have never been to can be a strange experience. You never know what to expect. The name of the school was *Modern Martial Arts* but I had also seen logos with *Fight Club* attached to the *Modern Martial Arts* name. I had looked up pictures of the school, and it looked like an MMA gym: a cage in one corner, boxing ring in the other, numerous heavy bags and an open mat space.

I have been to many martial arts schools. Sometimes the people are friendly, sometimes they are not. I didn't know anyone who trained at this place, so I was walking in blind. Each school has its own feel, and there is definitely a different vibe between a traditional martial arts school, a BJJ gym and an MMA gym.

There was a light snow coming down as I made my way from Pennsylvania. I crossed over the bridge into New Jersey, the Philly skyline off in the distance to my right. The day had come for my first Catch Wrestling lesson and I was on my way to meet Coach Joel Bane.

This would be a private lesson. I had no idea what to expect. The thought of a large wrestler slamming me on my head crossed my mind as I entered New Jersey. Catch

Wrestling had a nasty reputation. Its nickname was the *Violent Art.*

I had trained with plenty of martial artists over the years. I believed I could tell if a person was legitimate simply by training with them. I knew this person was a legit grappler simply because he was a Brazilian Jiu-jitsu Black Belt. But would he be able to teach me Catch Wrestling?

I found the gym and parked in the back parking lot, just as Coach Bane had instructed. A beat-up looking, old antique store stood behind the gym. The town itself seemed like a nice, quiet place.

I parked my car, stepped over an old rusty guard rail, and knocked on the back door to the gym. The door swung open and a man appeared. With a big smile he shook my hand and said, "I'm Joel, nice to meet you, brother!" He gestured for me to come inside.

He was a large man. My guess was 6'3" to 6'5", probably 250 to 275 pounds. Pure muscle, he didn't look like he had an ounce of fat on him. He wore wrestling shoes, blue athletic pants with a US Air Force logo on them, and a Snake Pit Catch Wrestling t-shirt.

Even with his intimidating stature, his friendly demeanor immediately disarmed me. I had met a lot of amazing fighters in my time though, and knew most of them seem like the nicest guys on earth off the mats. I changed my clothes and stepped into the gym.

I walked by the cage I had previously seen in pictures and onto the red and black mats. We had the entire place to ourselves. No one else was there. He briefly introduced himself, as did I, as we stretched out before the lesson.

He didn't believe in contracts, he explained, and I could come and train anytime I wanted to. It was also not that expensive. This was music to my ears, as that was one of my biggest problems with BJJ. You had to sign a long contract and it was pretty damn expensive.

He started pivoting on his knees and sitting out. He instructed me to follow him. I tried to replicate the half-circular movements. He did them as if it was second-nature.

We stood up and he grabbed my head in a chin-strap-like grip, and went through the details of how to snap someone down to the ground. Once on the ground, we began with a basic move I had done over and over again in Brazilian Jiu-jitsu, the top wrist-lock from side-control.

I felt like a building was on top of my chest as he lay on me. I knew he wasn't even trying to put all his weight on me, either. The details he went through on the move were insane, he dissected every minute little thing. His submission was extremely tight. I felt as if he left no room at all. Yet he managed to take the point of his elbow and dig it into my ribs while doing the movement. It was extremely painful…and again I knew he was being "nice." This use of the elbow to inflict pain on my ribs I had never experienced before in BJJ. It would have definitely been considered a "dirty" move.

While lying on me in side-control, he grasped his hands in an s-grip. His far arm had an under-hook while he gripped his top hand with the s-grip. While doing this, his top arm went over my jaw. He took the boney portion of his outside wrist and snagged it on my jaw. He cranked and I felt as though my jaw was going to be torn off.

He explained this was a "rip" and they have countless moves like this in Catch Wrestling. Catch Wrestlers like to use their knees, elbows and heads to inflict pain on their adversaries while grappling. They often refer to the outside bones of their arms from the elbow to the wrist and their shins as "cutting bones."

The lesson seemed to end as quickly as it started. I still had so many questions I wanted to ask, but was trying to absorb what I had just learned. The important thing, though, was that I had found someone I could learn from. I knew he could teach me what I wanted to know about Catch Wrestling. This lesson barely even scratched the surface.

As the months went by, I continued to make my way back to New Jersey. Sometimes alone, sometimes with my family in tow. My wife wanted to see where I was going. I wanted my three-year-old daughter to see the gym and watch the lessons. I believe you can learn a lot simply by observing.

The author and his daughter

Coach Bane took me through submission chains, an effective training technique Catch Wrestlers like to use. I found some submissions to be bizarre. Some that I had never seen before.

One such submission chain started with a “fisherman’s crank.” I thought I had seen most moves in the martial arts.

I mean, the body can move in only so many ways, but this was unique to me.

He started in side-control. He popped up and put his arm, specifically his elbow, vertically down my sternum in the middle of my chest, on my ribcage and stomach area. His other hand went behind my neck, the blade of his arm catching the back of my skull on the knowledge knot. He grasped his hands in an s-grip, his one elbow right beneath my xiphoid process.

He put his weight on my abdomen and chest while he sat-out and cranked my head toward my chest. The effect was a diaphragm choke and neck crank combined. It was a nasty move. He told me if you like the person, put your elbow below the xiphoid process. If you want to hurt the person, put the point of your elbow on the xiphoid process. When you crank it will break it off, or crack it well enough to cause discomfort for months.

The “nice” way of doing it will cause the person to choke as if they are drowning. There is no strangle on the neck, it is by directly compressing their lungs so that when they breathe out, they cannot take another breath in. If that doesn’t work for whatever reason, there is the neck crank as well.

Fisherman’s Crank

Keeping with the submission chain ideology, after the fisherman's crank, keep your s-grip with your hands. From this position you can slide right into a paper-cutter choke with some minor adjustments. This choke is an air-choke and is very painful for your opponent. Your arm stays behind his head while the other arm goes across his neck with the blade of your forearm. You clamp down with all your weight and apply the choke.

Paper-Cutter Choke

From here, keeping your s-grip, you sit up appearing to allow a way out for your opponent. He has nowhere else to go, so he will take the escape route you have seemingly given him. As he turns to escape, you slide your opposite arm under his chin, maintaining the same grip throughout and pull directly upward through the top elbow for the strangle hold. If he continues to move to his knees, you sit out past his shoulder. Then you drive your weight down while pulling up through his neck to secure the bulldog choke.

Transition to Strangle Hold (giving him what seems like an escape)

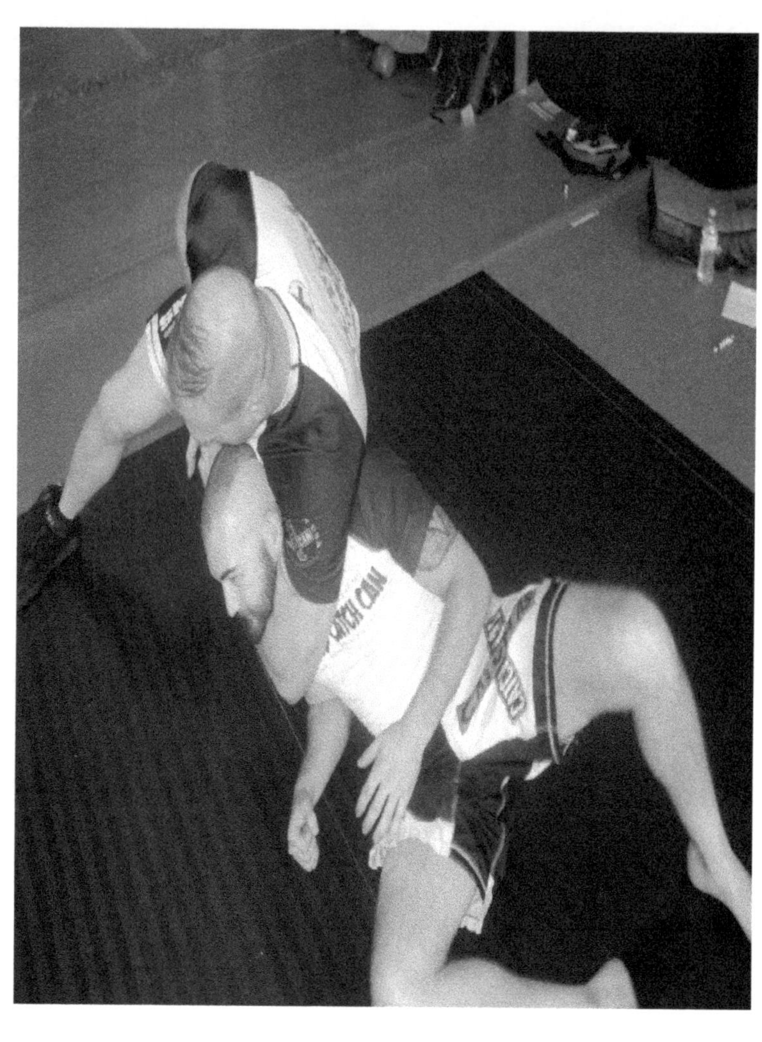

Sliding opposite arm under chin and rotating body—

transitioning to secure Strangle Hold

Strangle Hold

If your opponent is stubborn and does not submit, sit-out while doing the bulldog choke and apply your total weight. This is a vicious choke that often has an immediate effect.

Bulldog Choke

This is one of my favorite submission chains. It starts with the fisherman's crank. Then, you transition into a paper-cutter and strangle hold. Finally, you end with the bulldog choke. All the while, your hands never separate, keeping an s-grip.

Takedowns and defending takedowns are a big part of Catch Wrestling. One particular throw I was shown seemed interesting and quite effective: the "Half Halch Salto."

While standing up and wrestling, you get an underhook. You chinstrap your opponent with your one arm, while the arm with the underhook rides up as high as possible between the opponent's shoulders. The opponent's head should be trapped in your stomach area while you have the chinstrap.

You then sit back and toss your opponent directly over you, while keeping your grip on his head and your underhook. He will land on his back. You use the momentum of the throw to roll over your opponent and apply a nasty neck crank called a "cow catcher."

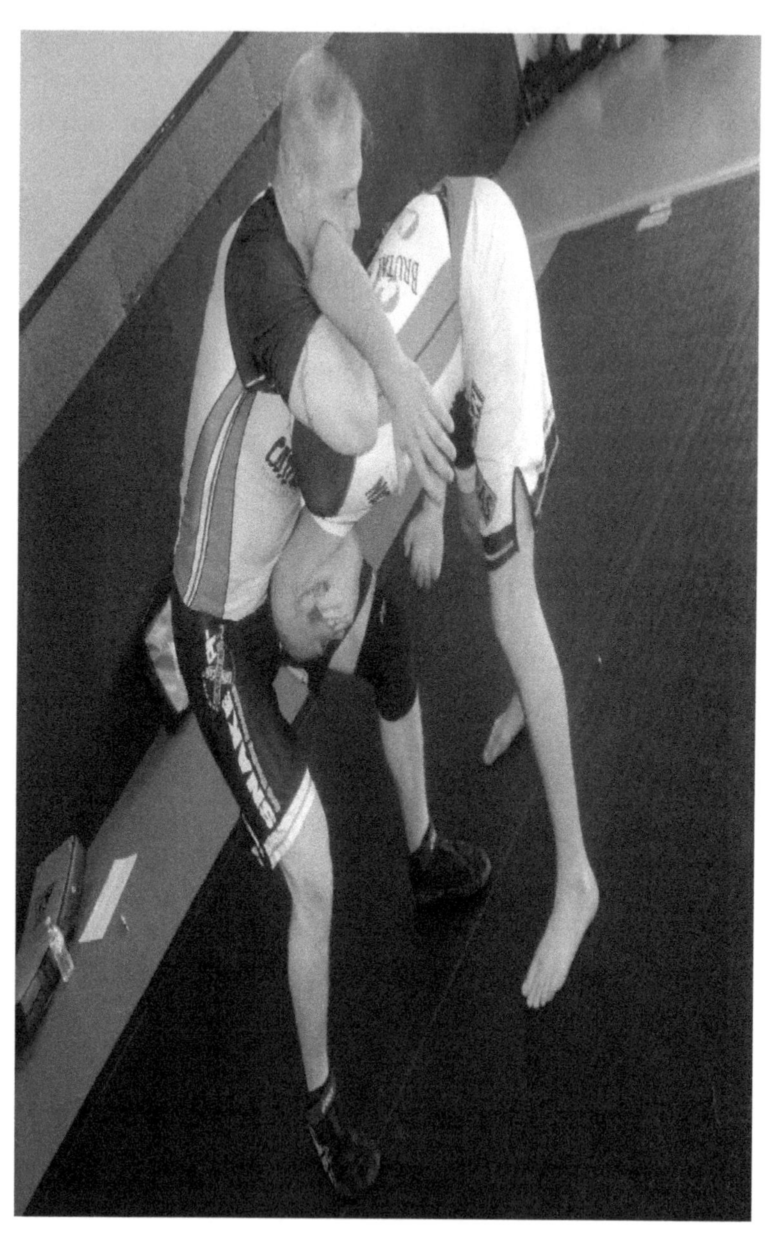

Half Halch Salto starting position

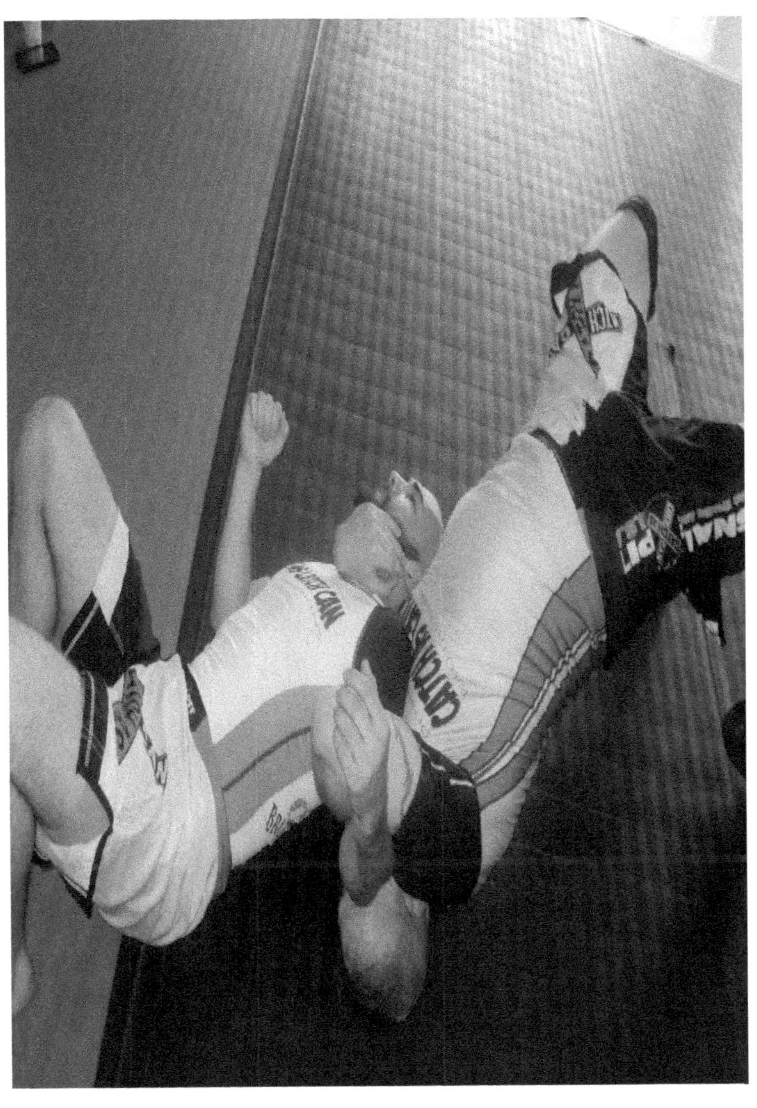

The sit and bridge to create the throw

Sit out to Cow Catcher Neck-Crank

Coach Bane also showed me the diaphragm choke I saw Josh Barnett use in his grappling match. The detail he went into was amazing. He wouldn't let me get away with making a single mistake. If the angle wasn't right and he didn't feel it, he would refuse to tap.

Even though I was smaller than him (and I am by no means a small guy) the technique worked. That was one misconception Coach Bane told me about Catch Wrestling, that it only works for big, strong guys. This couldn't be further from the truth, he said. He had many small students for whom the techniques worked just as well.

Coach Bane had already received his black belt in Brazilian Jiu-jitsu from Pat Stano, a former World Champion and black belt under the BJJ legend Sergio Penha. For those who don't already know, this is a huge achievement in the martial arts world. It usually takes a person at least ten years to achieve this.

He was also the Captain of the Wrestling Team for the United States Air Force for two years straight and had wrestled for the team for three years. All this coupled with his Catch Wrestling experience makes him an outstanding person to learn from.

The things I have listed above are just some of what I was taught. There are so many little details it is hard to discuss in a book. For instance, one is keeping your fingers tucked in and remaining aware of them, as they will get mangled during training for Catch. Funnily enough, I was taught the same thing while studying Japanese Jujutsu in Japan.

Coach Bane not only showed me the techniques, but let me crank them on him 100% full force. For example, we used the bulldog choke, which is a particularly nasty choke. He didn't want me applying it just halfway.

He would encourage me to crank the hell out of it and apply my full weight. I can still hear him yelling, "Whoa! You put some stank on that one!" I remember him saying how he felt his eye bulging out of his head and his face twitching.

Of course, it was to my benefit that he has a neck like a tree trunk, so I could go full force on him and make sure I was doing it correctly. If I wasn't, he would refuse to tap to it. It was the same with neck-cranks, he would let me crank the hell out of them, full force. I remember after one neck-crank him saying, "Did you hear my spine pop? Don't worry, I think you put it back in place!"

Having said this, he was as nice as could be to my daughter and wife. He would invite my daughter to play in the gym and would be particularly kind to her. My wife once needed to use the restroom and he immediately sprang up to his feet. "Hold on!" he said. "Not many women go in there, let me clean it up." We tried to tell him it was fine but he wouldn't listen and proceeded to clean it up before she entered.

I was glad I had found someone I could actually learn from. To me it seemed the Catch Wrestling was just part of the experience. Coach Bane really brought you in as if you were part of the family. My pregnant wife, daughter and I really appreciated that.

Chapter 4

Joel Bane

Expert Catch Wrestler Interview

June 12, 2016

It was a hot, sunny day in June when I traveled to Englishtown, New Jersey, to interview Coach Joel Bane. I sat down with him in the gym at *Modern Martial Arts*, the East Coast Headquarters of Snake Pit USA.

Coach Bane's wife and his understudy, Coach Brandon Browne, shared the mats with us while we delved into his life in the martial arts. I had no idea what the answers to the questions would be, but was eager to find out…

First of all, thank you for agreeing to do this interview. Could you start off by telling us a little bit

about yourself? How did you get involved in the martial arts and what's your lineage?

My name is Joel Bane and I'm thirty-six years old, I'll be thirty-seven very soon. I got involved in martial arts in 1999 when I was stationed in Wyoming. They didn't have much out there for martial arts or combat sports, so I drove down to Fort Collins, Colorado. I started training kickboxing with a friend of mine whom I actually worked with. It was not for fighting, really it was more for conditioning back then. There was a champion who trained at the gym. His dad was good, and they were from Thailand. We were more punching bags for him than anything else.

So, I did that for a little while and started Jiu-jitsu toward the end of that year on the campus at Colorado State University in '99. I stayed with Jiu-jitsu, purely Jiu-jitsu, until about 2006. I came to New Jersey in 2003. In 2006 I fought my first MMA fight. It was against a guy who was ranked number one. He was tied with Jeff Monson for grappling points across the nation and nobody would fight him, so I said I would. So, I fought him and I was doing fairly well. Even though I had a purple belt in Jiu-jitsu at the time and I felt like my Jiu-jitsu skills were pretty solid…he had takedowns, ground control and he was able to nullify a lot of my basic Jiu-jitsu transitions on the ground.

He wasn't very active, he was very…you know they talk about wrestlers sometimes how they have a tendency to stall, or lay and pray, he kind of did that. He wasn't a Catch guy or anything like that, but he did use good amateur wrestling. That was really the game-changer that fight. I ended up putting myself in a bad situation and actually beating myself, by getting impatient worrying about all the people who had come to watch me fight. We were fighting in the main event down in Wildwood, New Jersey. There were a couple thousand people watching and it was my first fight. I wasn't anxious that much but I felt like I didn't want to let anybody down. I kind of got impatient, moved the way I wasn't supposed to move, and I actually helped him finish a north-south choke. I can honestly say that I haven't been caught in a north-south choke, even in training, since then.

Those are the ones, when you lose, that you never get caught in again. When that happened I decided that Jiu-jitsu was not going to be enough. I didn't feel as if I was well-rounded enough. I thought that, although I could hit pretty hard even though my striking wasn't fancy, I knew I could take a hit and do what I needed to do to kind of start the grappling game. But I really didn't have much pummeling skill, takedown ability, ground control…the wrestling transitions were not there.

It was all a lot of transitions off the back, assuming that I'm going to my back. I really got tired of that mentality. That's not a knock on Jiu-jitsu, because I still do Jiu-jitsu. But it really kind of sent me in another direction.

Underhook and wrist control to the "Hank" takedown

So I started doing Catch Wrestling with a guy named Sean Daugherty. Sean was a UFC II vet, he was eighteen years old and fought in UFC II. He was actually "Big" John McCarthy's first "Let's get it on!" match that he refereed.

In that match, he was a kickboxing champion fighting some 6'8" ninja. He got choked out pretty quick because he didn't know any submissions. So Ken Shamrock grabbed him and Jason DeLucia up. He took them out to California as the first Lion's Den members. He taught them Catch Wrestling.

Sean joined the Air Force after 9/11 and we were stationed in the same place. We happened to come across each other in the same unit. Next thing you know we started working out together. I was very hesitant because I'm so picky about my coaches. I think lineage is everything. But he was an amazing coach. Probably the best philosopher as far as grappling goes whom I've ever met. He had a really good way of breaking things down...movement, transitions. Those were the things I really needed because that's the way I think about things.

I want to know why it works, how it works, why it's better. Prove me wrong if I say something else. So I trained with him for a while. A few years after I actually looked up this place, Modern Martial Arts, here in Englishtown, New Jersey. My current Snake Pit USA business partner, John Potenza, this was his home at the time. He was running the school.

So I came in here to bring my daughter to Judo and saw the CSW (Erik Paulson's Combat Submission Wrestling) logo on the wall and I'd seen the stuff with Billy Robinson online. Training with Billy Robinson was always something that I had wanted to do but it was very expensive. It was like over $1,000 not counting travel and lodging, to go train with the man. John had already trained with him a couple times so he was a little ahead of the curve with me on that. He had been with Erik for I think like thirteen or fourteen years at the time.

I started doing Erik Paulson seminars regularly and studying a lot of the CSW videos and really getting more involved in those. I already had a few of them I was studying a lot over the previous years. I kept trying to go to the Erik Paulson seminars and Greg Nelson seminars with John. As we started to go to the seminars together we became really good friends.

I had been coaching at a few places before. I was the head grappling coach at a couple other schools down near Philadelphia. To be honest, I kind of got tired of coaching. I kind of wanted to go back to being a student. That was my opportunity to go train under Billy and come here and work with John.

He actually helped me refine a couple of submissions. We drilled and worked out a lot together. That whole time I still trained with Sean off and on and I even ended up going back to Jiu-jitsu too—honestly to kind of finish something that I had started. Not because I thought it was better or anything, but because I love grappling, any kind of grappling that I can do, and I'm not adept to quitting anything.

So, I guess that's where it puts me today…

You recently received your black belt in Brazilian Jiu-jitsu?

I did. I also have a black belt in Shin Gi Tai Jujitsu, which is a modern Jujitsu program that is really just old-fashioned Judo with all the original ground fighting. I also hold a black belt in Judo. Coaches make all the difference. So, lineage is probably the most important thing. People don't want to train with me because I'm special. They want to train with me because my coaches were special. If I trained with bums, nobody would want to train with me. There's no reason.

So, obviously you're big on the Catch Wrestling scene. What exactly is Catch-as-Catch-Can Wrestling and where did it come from?

Catch Wrestling is…you always hear people defining it as "Catch anything you can." Webster's Dictionary actually defines it as "By any means available." Which is similar in meaning. Catch Wrestling started in the 1490s. You see this nonsense online for Wikipedia, which any fool can update, it says some guy name J.G. Chambers invented it in the late 1800s.

Attacking from Modified Side-Control with a one- arm submission chain

There were already Americans in the United States doing Catch Wrestling in the late 1800s. So, somebody in England wasn't making it up while somebody in the United States was doing it. The history, as I was taught face-to-face by Billy Robinson, that had been passed down to him by Billy Riley, was that at the end of the 1490s the British Empire started and Queen Elizabeth was ruling. She launched the Royal Navy off into South West Asia, down in India and all those areas like that.

Intro transition into the Wrestler's Guillotine

The sailors started bringing back all these different wrestling techniques. They refined them with the submission holds and things like that for hundreds of years. Billy Robinson told me a story one time; he was a big history buff. Another factor that gets overlooked is the influence of Greco Roman. Billy claimed the stance and clinch was heavily inspired by Greco, which is its elder style.

He was wrestling amateur and was wrestling some Turkish wrestlers. They kept doing what they called a leg-Turk. He went back to Billy Riley and he says, "Coach, they keep doing this leg-Turk." So he was like well, "Show it to me." He shows it to him and he kind of laughs at him.

He takes him down to his basement and there were these old books with drawings. These books were hundreds of years old. They were old Catch Wrestling books. There was a guy doing it (the leg-Turk), it's called a *Top-Ride.* "We've been doing it for quite some time. There is nothing new about it," Billy Riley explained.

There are no new techniques, they just get rediscovered. Catch Wrestling…we always say it's the

"Violent Art." I think it's the "Pure Art." It really is in the sense because it's not watered down. Someday it may get watered down as it keeps becoming more mainstream.

It's happened a lot with Jiu-jitsu, unfortunately. Right now it's our job to keep it pure with Snake Pit. That's really what we're trying to do by bringing good coaches in and keep it as pure as possible. People are usually blown away by all the submission holds. But the reason the submissions hurt is because we take out all that slack. Those little areas that are so important. We detail the crap out of everything, as much as humanly possible.

That's what usually blows away people the most. It's well rounded…doing Jiu-jitsu for all those years I didn't have takedowns. It was not until I started studying wrestling and Judo at the same time. Where are the takedowns coming from? How are we "miracle-ing" it to the ground? I'm not pulling guard. I'd rather get thrown on my head than pull guard. I really would. I don't care if I'm sixty…I'm not pulling guard. If I get taken down, I get taken down. It doesn't happen very often, but oh well, if it does, I'm not pulling guard.

That ain't fightin'. One thing that's really changed is Jiu-jitsu was feared in the early 1900s and Catch Wrestling was very sport-like. Nowadays Jiu-jitsu is very sport-like and Catch Wrestling is feared. So times have changed a little bit. You see a lot more of the fighters go toward the Catch Wrestling.

There are no illegal holds. It's a style that always embraced every single hold. The term "No Holds Barred" comes from Catch Wrestling in the early 1900s. Guys want to practice a style that doesn't limit them. So, that makes sense.

Why have you decided to focus your energy on teaching Catch Wrestling?

Well, I teach everything. I teach Jiu-jitsu and Catch Wrestling. I've taught a lot of Judo and even MMA sometimes. Catch is my favorite because it's the most pure in form, I believe it's the most well-rounded. I started studying Catch Wrestling because I wanted to round out my Jiu-jitsu game. Then I realized it was actually the other way around.

I realized that Catch Wrestling does a full circle back to everything. Everything ties in so well, it just makes sense. Everything you do, you'd be like oh my gosh, why didn't I think of that. Little adjustments here, little adjustments there, even after all the years of Jiu-jitsu. Everything makes sense.

You can see people when they come into a Catch Wrestling class, guys who have been doing Jiu-jitsu fifteen years, who haven't been exposed to it. They see the Catch Wrestling techniques and their eyes get big. It gets exciting and it's very addictive.

It's well-rounded and honestly there's so much Jiu-jitsu out there. It wouldn't do anybody a lot of good to put up another Jiu-jitsu business, when we can offer something not everybody can get to.

So, exactly how is it different from Brazilian Jiu-jitsu?

The biggest difference is the takedowns and control. Most of the positions are the same. There are some different names. We don't utilize things like a half-guard very much or anything like that. I guess you could call it a "half body scissors", we don't really utilize that very often. You can use it as long as you're not getting pinned.

The Wrestler's Guillotine submission and pin

It is a bit more aggressive. The thing I teach a lot, and John does the same thing…is most of our guys are confident in getting off their back, instead of comfortable lying on their back all day. I want my students confident on their backs, not comfortable. Confident they can quickly escape the position or submit their opponent. You know, that's not somewhere I want to be in an altercation. We don't necessarily train for sport. We train for life-threatening situations and things like that.

You were a Captain of the United States Air Force Wrestling Team. Could you tell us about that experience?

I was on the team for three years and I was the Captain for the last two. I used to teach the Army combative guys on Fort Dix for years. I trained them for tournaments, along with Sean Daugherty for a while. When Sean left, I took over training those guys, the level four guys.

Then the Air Force Wrestling Team came to the base. I didn't know there was an Air Force Wrestling Team, to be honest. My first wrestling coach, before I lost that first MMA fight, was an amateur wrestler named Santos Caban. He was an All-American Wrestler whom I owe a ton of credit to, but I had never really trained *specifically* amateur wrestling.

So, the wrestling experience I had was Catch Wrestling and some with my buddy Santos for a few years. When the Air Force Team came out to Fort Dix to train, they had only one real heavyweight. They usually had wrestle-offs at every weight class but there was only one heavyweight and there was nobody to wrestle him. So the Army guys were like, why don't you have Bane in here? And they were like, "Well, who's that?"

So I kept getting all these phone calls and emails to come wrestle or to come try out or something. I had never wrestled pure Greco or pure Freestyle. It was always Catch or some form of broken submission wrestling, then mixed with Catch with Sean.

I just had surgery. I had my biceps reattached, my collarbone cut and my labrum repaired about four weeks before. So I came into wrestling with a sling on. The wrestling coach at the time looked at me like I was crazy, but he was pretty crazy too and he said “Let’s do it!”

I literally took off the sling the next day and duct taped my arm to my side. I ended up wrestling at the US Open in Las Vegas for the team a month later. I started studying Freestyle and Greco under Floyd “Bad News” Winter for the next few years. Coach Winter was the first American ever to win Gold in Greco in the World Championships. He was also a former Greco National Champion, Sambo National Champion, 2-time Olympic Coach and trainer of Randy Couture, not to mention several Olympians. His accolades really do go on forever. He’s the best and has been like a father to me. He really stepped in when we lost Coach Robinson.

So I had the best I could have asked for in a Freestyle/Greco coach. Coach Winter went from being team manager to Head Coach in my second year and asked me to come back one more year to be Captain, so I did. I did three years of that with the team.

Most of the time I was injury riddled. I got to the amateur wrestling when I was a little too old. There was already so many years of damage from the military and combat sports training. I was probably about ten years too late as far as All-American type titles or anything like that.

Honestly, I think they used me more of as a technician and a team leader because there wasn't a whole lot left of my body. We had some good death matches and some great workouts and we pushed it as hard as we could at the National Championships and the Armed Forces Championships.

So, you're a heavyweight. What do you normally walk around at?

I usually walk around about 240 pounds. Well, I should be walking around at about 240 pounds, I'm probably about 245 right now. When I wrestled for the Air Force, the first year, I was only about 225 to 230 pounds because I had those surgeries. The second year I was about 270 pounds.

The third year, I wrestled with two herniated discs and I ripped two tendons off my hamstring. The leg is still deformed in the back. I couldn't work out much so I dropped down to about 255 to 260 pounds. Normally, right now, coaching and working out with the guys I'm probably about 240 to 245pounds.

Could you tell us about your military career?

Sure. I joined the Air Force in 1997. I joined as a Security Forces member. My first job was Nuclear Weapons Security, basically guarding silos in Wyoming. My career field was split at the time. There was air base defense side, which was more ground combat skills than the other side, which is law enforcement based. I've never done one day of law enforcement in my career.

When I joined, I actually didn't know it was related to law enforcement in any way. They took me to the school and they were like "Welcome to the Security Forces building," and I see all these badges. I was like what the…I'm at the wrong place!

I did the Security Specialist Airbase defense stuff and did a lot of great training with the Army. I did a lot of Army schools, Sniper schools, training in combative schools, close-quarter combat schools, Air Assault, Path Finder and places like that. I've been very fortunate to be assigned to a lot of combat-oriented units.

I was assigned to the Contingency Response Wing on McGuire where I set up the sniper program for the Air Force. They call it the *Sharpshooter Program*, it's the exact same thing designed off the Army and Marine Corps courses.

I've been deployed six times. Three times to Afghanistan, one time to Iraq, and two more times to Saudi Arabia. I taught combatives in Afghanistan and Iraq to Coalition and US Forces. That was more when I had time, it wasn't my primary duty or anything like that. Force Protection was always my main duty for both on and off base.

In 2011 I returned from my last deployment and started working on Fort Dix. Now I analyze ground combat data for the Air Force. Everybody thinks that everyone flies in the Air Force but pilots make up only a couple percent of the Air Force.

Whether it's Special Operations, Army or Security Forces, I take that data and basically filter through it and disseminate it out, what needs to be sent out. Like if a tactic is working well against enemy personnel, we basically take that, refine it, and send it out.

That's really interesting stuff. Thank you for your service to our country.

Sure, thank you.

Getting back to Catch Wrestling, who exactly was Billy Robinson and what did he mean to Catch Wrestling? What impact did he have on you?

When I started learning Catch Wrestling with Sean, I knew who Karl Gotch was. I kind of loosely heard Billy's name thrown around, but I didn't know much about him. I'm a history geek so I started kind of researching more of the Catch stuff.

I kept coming across Kazushi Sakuraba, who is probably the most popular Catch wrestler ever—and Billy Robinson trained him. So if he's the best, and Billy trained him, I thought that would be the way to go.

I never met anybody else from the original Snake Pit, but most say he was the best technician who ever came out of the original Snake Pit. That is of course the home of *Catch Wrestling*. He said one guy was better than him, Billy Joyce aka Bob Robinson, but obviously I never met him so I wouldn't know.

Japanese Armbar (Note: Opponent's thumb MUST be turned down toward their feet to shut down any chance of a bridging escape)

But most people consider Billy (Robinson) the best technician who ever came out of there. *He was Catch Wrestling*. At the time before his death, if you thought about Catch Wrestling, you knew who Billy Robinson was.

If you trained any type of Catch Wrestling you had to know who Billy was. He would be as Helio Gracie is to Gracie Jiu-jitsu. It technically started with Carlos Sr. but everybody thinks of Helio, right? Well, Billy is the same way. Everybody thinks of Billy when you think of Catch Wrestling, even now that he's gone.

I know you have competed in numerous martial arts events including MMA (Mixed Martial Arts) and grappling. Could you tell us of any fights that stick out in your mind and why?

I guess they're all kind of weird in their own way. My first MMA fight I wanted to put on a show, I didn't try to develop a career in any way. I wasn't very smart. I wanted to fight the best or biggest every time I did anything. I felt people were coming to watch, so let's make it interesting.

If I hadn't lost that first fight, we wouldn't be sitting here right now doing this interview, and Snake Pit USA wouldn't exist. There's no way. I'm a sore loser, I don't like losing at all—I despise it. It really pissed me off for a long time that I had lost.

I wanted to find the biggest thing I could for my second fight, so I found a three-hundred pounder and choked him out. But that first fight was really the game-changer.

In 2013 I did the World Grappling Team trials in Vegas at the National Championship/US Open. I wrestled Brandon Ruiz. That was of course right after my surgeries.

I'm not making any excuses, he absolutely beat me fair and square for the title. I guess I knew in the back of my head I didn't stand a chance because I had only one arm and I hadn't been training submissions for a few months.

What do you mean by you had one arm?

My left arm was completely useless. This was less than two months after collar bone, labrum and biceps surgery and nothing had really healed due to Air Force Wrestling camp, where I was convinced I had re-torn the biceps. Maybe it was ego…perhaps I needed to be reminded I'm not as invincible as I once thought I was.

They still let you fight like that?

I didn't tell them. I don't know if it was arrogance or what, but I think the good Lord chose to humble me. So, I went out there…I knew I wasn't going to be able to pummel with him because I know he's like a seven or eight time All-American at Greco and Freestyle.

I thought if I got to the ground I could get a leg pretty easy and still be able to finish it. That was silly of me to think that but it was a good learning experience. I think you learn more from your losses than you do your wins.

I've had plenty of wins in grappling tournaments. Most of them were very quick. You have good days and bad days. Billy Robinson told me once that Billy Riley said, "You have to learn how to lose, or you'll never appreciate winning. You won't be able to continue training effectively." If you can't accept loss the right way you're never going to be worth a crap.

Many athletes who train in MMA and grappling for any length of time suffer from injuries. How has your body held up through the years of brutal training? Do you have any tips for staying healthy while training?

My body's pretty trashed, to be completely honest. It's hard to really differentiate what's from what. I've been in the military almost nineteen years. I've definitely had a lot of injuries going through Army courses and training myself for those courses.

I've pushed myself really, really hard with my military career going to those schools. I was supposed to switch service branches into the Army and do the SFAS program, the Special Forces Assessment Selection phase.

I tortured my body for two years straight preparing for that and other Army courses and training other guys. I think that did a lot of damage to certain joints that just aren't right anymore.

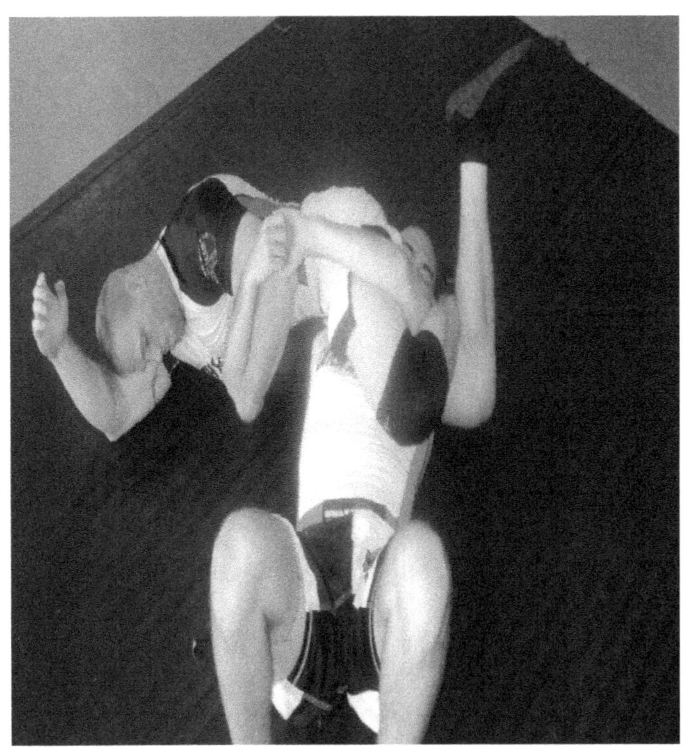

Inverted Triangle from Armbar defense

As far as grappling goes, the knees are pretty torn up. My elbows, my hands, some of it's…honestly, it's a tough question to answer. You don't know what's genetic and what's not. I know my arthritis and tendinitis and stuff like that are genetic.

I know the herniated disc stuff is probably from strength training and lifting too heavy when I was too young. My first surgeries were all from grappling. Torn cartilage, torn rotator cuff, torn labrums, both knees.

When I first started learning heel hooks, I learned not to get caught in them by my knee getting torn off. That's how I learned. Sean was my Catch coach and he came from Ken Shamrock. The Lion's Den mentality was if you get caught in it you get it torn off pretty much or you go out when you get choked. You learn not to get caught in it again out of fear. Fear is the greatest motivator.

That's a rough style of training…

It definitely is. There's definitely a price to pay. If you really want to do it and train hard enough. I remember doing two a days for about four years straight with grappling. That probably took the biggest toll on me.

During that time, as far as pure grappling, I probably over-trained. I didn't take very good care of myself.

If I could do it again…honestly the only thing I would change is actually going to the doctor. I refused to go to the doctor for anything. I don't know how much difference that would have made, because I wouldn't change the way I trained.

I would change the way I took care of myself. A lot more ice. I didn't use it at all. I don't know why, that was foolish. It obviously makes a big difference. I was just used to being sore all the time and just really didn't care.

Would you say that Catch Wrestling is an optimal combat art for modern-day MMA? How about self defense in a street situation?

I think it's the best single form. For both of those. I think the application makes perfect sense. We fight to stay off our back and if we go to our back we're ready. We can get off our back better than anybody. We do takedowns that have the potential to knock somebody out by themselves.

The pummeling is off the charts. We do the highest level pummeling possible. The takedowns are basic and simple and destructive. They are combined with submissions that…just the concept alone of control. If my first priority is control, I'm already one step ahead of any adversary on the street or in a fight.

The pummeling control, the ground control, any positional control, it's all based on controlling your opponent. Catch Wrestling is more offensive than it is defensive because of the concept of control. If I'm controlling you, I'm not terribly concerned with your attacks because you're spending your entire time running from me.

I've had guys come up to me after grappling tournaments and actually say that. They're , man, in a friendly way, I really felt like I was trying to counter you the whole time. I really couldn't get my game going. So, it's kind of the idea that if I did that then I'm doing the right thing.

I'm attacking. I'm not waiting for a mistake, I'm trying to cause a reaction. Sometimes them running for their lives leaves things hanging out. In Jiu-jitsu, a lot of times we train low level guys and white belts to "Wait for them to make a mistake, wait for them to make a mistake."

We're not training for joe blow on the street. We should be training to take on the world champion, to train at the highest level possible. With Catch Wrestling having unlimited submissions, no illegal holds, and the pummeling combined with the takedowns mixes better with striking than any other form of grappling.

Nobody else really pushes that. What connects your grappling to your striking? Catch being as well-rounded as it is just makes perfect sense to me.

Why have so many people never heard of Catch Wrestling? Why aren't there more people training in it? Is it martial arts politics or is there something else at play?

Catch Wrestling has never been marketed in the same way as other styles. It was probably the number one sport in the United States in the early 1900s. A lot of guys protected it because it was the way they earned a living. If I taught you, and you got better than me, it might cost me my job someday.

So, they didn't want their techniques out there?

Not that it was secret or anything like that, but it wasn't like they were in a bunch of gyms selling their techniques.

Common sense…

Absolutely, it has never been marketed heavily because it kind of fizzled out with television. The real guys being told they had to lose weren't too keen on that with a thirty-minute time slot. So they had to start picking guys who were willing to go in there and play the game. A lot of the real grapplers got phased out.

You covered a lot, just curious if there is martial arts politics involved, etc.?

I don't think it's politics so much. I don't think anybody is trying to stop it. It is hard to…I think we're the first ones who have come along and really put a lot of monetary effort into it.

You guys seem to be doing seminars all over the place.

Almost every weekend. It funds itself in a way, but we put our money into it all the time too, John and I. All the money we make pretty much goes back into Snake Pit to keep pushing it into further growth with its merchandise, DVDs, seminars, etcetera. We take it on ourselves to carry that flag. There's been a lot of people over the years who have attempted it, but they really just didn't have the monetary ability.

They didn't have the funds to do it. I think Jake Shannon did a great job with Scientific Wrestling and he still does a great job.

I know Erik Paulson mixes a lot of Catch Wrestling with his style and a lot of people embrace that and love the Catch Wrestling that he does within the CSW program.

We are getting ready to launch a campaign nationwide over the next few weeks actually. We're going after gyms as affiliates. That will be the first time we've done that.

We've had twenty some gyms sign up at one time or another, but that's all people coming to us, haphazardly. So, we're going to start going after those gyms and locations.

So you're really trying to spread out?

Absolutely. People get scared of Catch Wrestling because everybody pushes the "Violent Art, Violent Art." People don't want to bring in their five-year-old kid to practice the "Violent Art." What it really is…is real submission wrestling with very detailed technique.

It's not necessarily more dangerous than any other style, but the Violent Art label does scare people off sometimes. Some guys want to train to get into shape, some guys want to train for this or that. That's why you see a lot of the fighters go toward Catch and steer a little bit away from Jiu-jitsu.

A lot of the guys looking to get into shape and learn some self defense are doing a lot more of the Jiu-jitsu style now, at least that's what I've seen.

Honestly, if people don't know what *Catch Wrestling* is, I don't understand it. For me to go forward I have to know where I've come from, which makes me want to study history. So, for me to get into a hobby and devote any time to it I would like to know something about it…actually study it and where it came from and what it's about. That's how I found Catch Wrestling.

I was doing Jiu-jitsu and I started studying grappling and learning the history of the styles. If you are doing Jiu-jitsu you are doing some form of Catch Wrestling at some point. Because Jiu-jitsu is influenced heavily by Judo and Catch Wrestling from Mitsuyo Maeda. He did them both.

If you don't know what Catch Wrestling is, you don't know your history. That's really all there is to it.

Where do you see Catch Wrestling headed in the future? What would you like to say to that person who would like to pick up Catch Wrestling to improve their fighting skills?

Catch is going to continue to grow. It will get big. Anybody doing combat sports will know what it is. I don't think it will ever be as big as Gracie Jiu-jitsu. The reason I say that is it's a little bit rougher.

Not necessarily…technique-wise…I guess the application of the techniques. Not that you have to do it with bad intentions, but it is meant to cause pain. It's meant to get someone to quit.

We do crossfaces. Recently one of our coaches was told by some other Jiu-jitsu coach that his kid's a dirty fighter because he crossfaced a kid. It wasn't in the rules that he can't. To me that's good grappling.

He's doing what he's supposed to do. There's nothing wrong with that, but as long as there's that stigma that it's dirty, it's not going to be as popular. You know when people call things dirty in grappling, usually it's something pure and just a bit more than some can handle. It's what it is supposed to be.

It's not about sport, it's really not.

What would you like to say to that person who is hesitant to step into the gym and train in Catch Wrestling?

I usually explain to them it really is the only *real* submission wrestling. You see submission wrestling at every gym. They say No-Gi this, No-Gi that, well guess what—Judo has a Gi and so does Jiu-jitsu.

As soon as you take off that Gi you're either doing…I don't know Lord knows what…I think Josh Barnett said once either you're doing Catch Wrestling or some other sloppy thing, whatever you think it is.

There is no other style without the Gi really. Other than Lucha Libre which is just a hybrid style of Catch Wrestling. Helio Gracie himself said Jiu-jitsu is with a Gi. So, I don't understand why No-Gi Jiu-jitsu classes happen today. I really don't. It doesn't make any sense to me.

If the guy who supposedly created the system, says it is with a Gi you don't get to just change that years later. You don't get to say no, no it's not.

I tell them it's submission wrestling. It's the purest form of submission wrestling. It's the only real form of submission wrestling. It's Catch-as-Catch-Can style. It's the only popular style that actually has techniques devoted 100% to No-Gi.

The Cobra Choke

You want to be an MMA fighter? Guess what? You don't wear a Gi in the cage. If you want to fight on the street, guess what? You don't know what you'll be wearing that day. You might not be able to utilize your outfit as a weapon. There are just no limits to the Catch Wrestling application like there are other grappling styles.

Catch makes the most sense. It's not that hard to market if you know what it really is. Some people struggle. They put Catch-as-Catch-Can up and it confuses people. Not everyone is going to go google it. Most people searching martial arts gyms do know what submission wrestling is.

It has to be packaged a certain way. If you can explain it as submission grappling for MMA or No-Gi submission grappling for MMA, then kind of say, "Hey! Guess what we're doing, guys? It's Catch Wrestling!" Then people are like, "Holy crap, I love it."

I mean you've done it. It's very addictive.

Yeah, it's definitely addictive. It's a lot of fun too; it's very different. I would like to thank you again for agreeing to this interview. Do you have any last comments you would like to add?

Yeah, go join *Team Snake Pit USA* and become a part of this great Catch Wrestling Revolution!

Chapter 5

A History Lesson

When it comes to the martial arts, Catch Wrestling has proven that the grass is not always greener on the other side. Sometimes what you are looking for is staring you right in the face.

If you are looking for an effective, proven form of martial art to use in a fight or defend your family, you don't need to travel all the way to Asia. You don't need to delve into the endless list of exotic martial arts based on myths and legends.

If your main concern is simply fighting, look no further than Catch Wrestling. It is one of the earliest forms of MMA and has been battle tested for centuries. It has been used in no-holds-barred fights all around the world with great success.

Many of the same moves you see nowadays in MMA fights have been in Catch Wrestling's repertoire for ages. Moves that look complicated that are believed to come from Eastern Asia have long been used by the Catch Wrestler. Take for instance a "kimura" or "ude garami" lock often used in modern-day grappling. In Catch it is called a "double wrist-lock" and is one of their go-to bread-and-butter moves.

Double Wrist-Lock (Note: Coach Bane's thumb around wrist/thumb-less grip is ONLY for transition to short arm scissor; the double wrist-lock is normally performed with a full thumb grip since Catch Wrestlers do not wear Gis)

Who invented it first? That nobody will ever know. Could have been the Egyptians, could have been the Greeks. However, Catch guys were using it long before it ever became popular. It wasn't some super-secret move from Japan or China, that came from a hermit living in a cave who studied anatomy. It was used by Catch guys because it made their opponents submit. In short, it simply *worked.*

It is said that legendary Catch Wrestler Billy Robinson never liked the idea of fighting off your back in MMA. He emphasized getting off your back, as being there is very dangerous while in a fight. He had a lifetime of fighting experience that told him this. Even though fighting off your back had become popular in MMA, he disagreed with it.

Sure enough, as MMA evolved you saw far fewer people fighting off their backs. His words seemed prophetic. He was an elderly man watching young men fight in an ever-evolving sport, yet he seemed to know exactly where the sport was headed.

It is said that history often repeats itself. If you are a student of the martial arts, specifically MMA and grappling, you should take notice of Catch Wrestling's history.

Many people see modern-day MMA as something new. For instance, it is widely believed that few knew about how important ground fighting was until MMA came to America in the 1990s. This couldn't be further from the truth.

While it is true many people who studied traditional Asian martial arts did not know about this (except for maybe some Judo players), Catch Wrestlers always knew this. It wasn't just the BJJ guys who realized learning what positions were dominant on the ground would often lead to a victory—not to mention other grapplers such as Sambo practitioners, traditional wrestlers, and so on.

However, at the beginning of MMA in America in the 1990s, Catch Wrestling didn't have much of a platform. Few people knew about it. In modern MMA, more and more fighters are gravitating toward Catch Wrestling because of its proven effectiveness. It is a dominating and aggressive art. It is meant for fighting.

Looking at Catch Wrestling's history is interesting. It started out as the go-to art for fighting in no-holds-barred competitions and MMA style matches. There were different schools and each had its own specialties. Men would fight to make extra money to feed their families.

It drew larger and larger crowds and became very popular. It was a risky business though, as injuries were commonplace.

Fighters risked a lot stepping into the ring. Anything could happen, especially when there were few to no rules and weight classes didn't exist. In the end, it was all about pleasing the crowds. That is where the money came from.

If two evenly matched fighters stepped into the ring and the fight went to the ground, it could become quite boring for the average fan who paid to watch. The fight on the ground could go on for a very, very long time.

As the years went on and television was introduced, promoters realized there was an easier way. What if the fights were pre-arranged in an entertaining way? The crowds would not be privy to this and they could eliminate all that boring ground fighting. It would also avoid many of the injuries often associated with a real fight.

Over time Catch Wrestling was phased out. As with many martial arts, the real and effective techniques were lost in the sands of time. This happened with numerous Asian martial arts in times of peace. The techniques were replaced with rituals.

In Catch Wrestling's history, it's really not all that different. Instead of rituals, wrestling simply turned into entertainment. The result is the same, however. The *real* techniques, and *real* fighters, were lost somewhere along the way.

It all makes perfect sense when you step back and look at it from a distance. Why risk life and limb when you can make more money simply pretending to do the same thing? It mimicked the traditional martial arts in times of peace. It simply was not needed.

I personally believe that injuries to the fighters played a major role. Even in modern MMA and grappling, you will hear people say that it is no more dangerous than any other sport. You get injuries in all sports they say, including football, baseball, soccer, and so on.

I couldn't disagree more. Sure, you get injuries in other sports. I played many sports when I was younger including baseball, football and soccer. The difference between these sports and MMA/grappling is that nobody is trying to knock you out, break your limbs or choke you unconscious.

While wear and tear in traditional sports can lead to injury and of course the occasional hard blow, MMA and grappling are different. For instance, while grappling you are constantly having your joints over-extended. This is how arm-locks, leg-locks and neck-cranks work.

The wear and tear of this over time can lead to serious injury. Even more so can be the accidental hyperextension that leads to a broken limb. Or perhaps you are rolling or training with a partner who dislikes you for whatever reason. They can simply ignore your tap and break your limb, choke you unconscious or body slam you with the intent of doing serious injury. Broken teeth, broken limbs and concussions are a real possibility when training.

There is a big difference between playing a sport and training in combat sports where the other person wants to inflict harm upon you. To me, the people who say that the martial arts are just as safe as other sports are using a sales gimmick. They are not.

They can be made *safer* by finding good training partners. However, the moves are inherently dangerous and accidents can and do happen.

The resurgence of MMA into the public eye has once again captivated the masses. Just as with Catch Wrestling back in the day, people are eager to see men battle it out in hand-to-hand combat. This MMA revolution has also breathed new life into the almost forgotten art of Catch

Wrestling. Almost completely lost, people like Joel Bane and John Potenza of Snake Pit USA are pushing for a comeback.

Because of people like them and their efforts, Catch Wrestling is rising out of the ashes. It seems to be coming full-circle: from an extremely effective form of combat, to almost disappearing with fixed pro-wrestling matches, to once again being sought after by professional modern-day MMA fighters.

MMA is a global phenomenon now. Fights are being held all over and people everywhere are practicing it.

However, large MMA promoters have already limited the time a fight can stay on the ground to please the crowds. Weight classes have become mandatory and more and more rules keep being added along with shorter time limits. In certain areas, MMA fights are not allowed because it is seen as too brutal of a sport.

Much of this seems reminiscent of what happened to Catch Wrestling and its pre-MMA no-holds-barred fights. We are at a time now when society (most of society) is willing to have these modern-day Mixed Martial Arts cage matches on television. There is a big enough fan base, and most importantly, enough money to justify the fights.

How long will society allow these fights to happen this go around? It is becoming a well-established sport, but I feel more and more rules will be added to continue its growth and acceptance. To be accepted by the mainstream, it will have to continually be watered down.

When injuries happen in the cage such as someone getting their leg or arm broken, it makes people cringe. Recently there was a fighter who was kneed in the head. He had the bones in the front of his skull broken, causing a gruesome indentation. This was a major MMA fight and the injury made headlines around the world.

These men and women stepping into the cage are warriors, no doubt. In most fights there are no serious, lasting injuries. However, the serious injuries are the ones that make the headlines. I wonder how long the sport of MMA will last. It will most likely depend on how the public at large sees it.

Will MMA eventually go the route Catch Wrestling did and turn into staged matches? Who knows.

Catch Wrestling literally almost went extinct.

As a martial art, we are lucky it has survived to this day. The only reason it did is that men were willing to sacrifice their time and bodies to preserving the art.

Times are changing along with technology. In the past, knowledge was passed from teacher to student. If you were lucky, someone wrote it down in a book somewhere.

In modern times we have film and the internet. All of these MMA fights are being recorded, saved for posterity.

You can go on YouTube and spend endless amounts of time researching the martial arts and techniques. Could you imagine if we had film from ancient fights in Greece, Rome, Japan and the rest of the world? I bet it would change the way we look at the martial arts and fighting.

Snake Pit USA has made numerous videos preserving Catch-as-Catch-Can techniques for future generations.

There is no replacement for a real, qualified teacher. However, in the case where history repeats itself and Catch Wrestling and MMA go underground again, this information will always be there, available for someone to pick up the torch again.

My journey into the martial arts has been a long and strange one. I have gone from one extreme to another. I have studied traditional martial arts in Asia, sword and knife fighting in Latin America, Brazilian Jiu-jitsu, Catch Wrestling and MMA.

Every martial art I have studied seeks the same answer. How do I defeat another man in combat? Sometimes the answer has been more psychological than physical. Other times, it is pure savage violence. Each art approaches it differently.

With the state of the martial arts in the world today, you have various schools vying for a piece of the pie. The major players are the traditional martial arts schools, BJJ and MMA gyms. However, Catch Wrestling is pushing its way back in and rightly so.

I have confidence that no matter where the martial arts and MMA head in the future, Catch Wrestling will be there and a part of it. Its history and combat effectiveness is undeniable.

With many people heading away from traditional martial arts and steering toward MMA, Catch has a perfect opening for a comeback.

For the history buffs, which many of the traditional martial artists are, Catch has more than enough to offer. Just as many Japanese martial arts took techniques from China and made them their own, so did Catch with Asia and the Middle East.

English sailors went to far off, exotic lands and learned wrestling and fighting techniques. They went to India and the Middle East, bringing back techniques from styles such as Pehlwani from India and Pahlavani from Iran.

They mixed this with their English wrestling and came up with *Catch*. Even though Catch Wrestling is a straightforward, no-nonsense form of wrestling and fighting, it has some pretty interesting roots. Other English styles noted for their contribution to the development of Catch Wrestling are Lancashire, Cornish, Devonshire, Cumberland and Westmorland. Then there are a couple other European styles that also influenced its development such as Irish Collar-and-elbow and Greco Roman.

Until recently, most people associated martial arts with the mysteries and enchantments of Asia. MMA changed that to a certain extent. However, most still like to think of the martial arts in terms of kung fu movies with high spinning kicks and karate chops.

Some of us however, now have a different picture of the martial arts. It looks something like this*: a heavyset, brawny European man from the 1800s, with no shirt, tights, and wearing wrestling shoes. He sports a thick mustache, ox-like neck and a mean stare. He is a Catch Wrestler and will throw down with anyone who dares.*

2◄
PV
2◄
AD13_C001
180.0
25ft

About the Author

Daniel DiMarzio was born on the Army Base in Fort Campbell, Kentucky, in 1982. He graduated from Peirce College in 2006 with a Bachelor of Science in Business Administration, Concentration in Management, and is a member of Delta Mu Delta, International Honor Society in Business Administration. He is also a graduate of the Pennsylvania School of Muscle Therapy.

Daniel is the author of numerous books investigating cultures around the world.

His books are available in stores worldwide. They can also be found in public libraries from Dubai to Kathmandu and beyond.

Books by Daniel DiMarzio

Stay Low and Circle Left, The Story of Floyd "Bad News" Winter

Daniel puts an American War Hero and All Army Wrestling legend's story down on paper for future generations.

Igor Vovchanchyn, The King of Fighting

Daniel travels to Kharkiv, Ukraine, on the border of Russia near the ongoing conflict. There he meets Igor "Ice Cold" Vovchanchyn, one of the most legendary and feared MMA and No Holds Barred fighters of all-time.

From Machete Fights to Paradise: The Machete Fighters of the Dominican Republic

Do you think sword fights are a thing of the past? Think again. Daniel travels to areas of the Dominican Republic rarely ever seen by the non-local to investigate.

Catch Wrestling, Stepping into the Snake Pit

Daniel's journey training and learning about the history of catch-as-catch-can wrestling with legendary coach Joel Bane.

www.ingramcontent.com/pod-product-compliance
Ingram Content Group UK Ltd.
Pitfield, Milton Keynes, MK11 3LW, UK
UKHW022018190726
13853UKWH00005B/1995

9 798703 390528